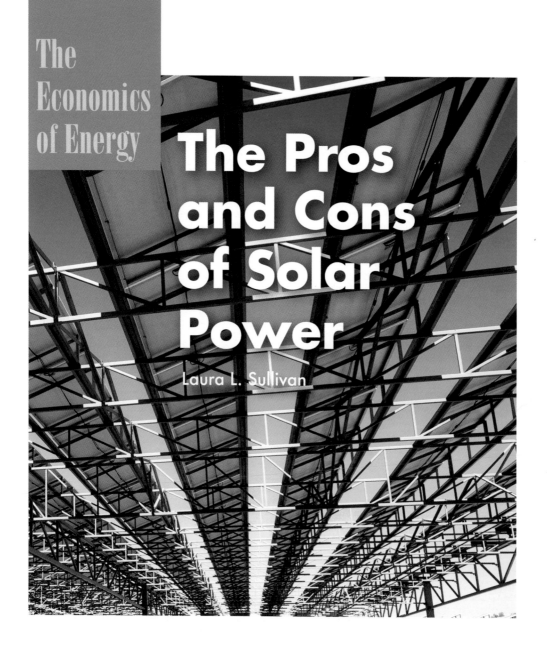

The Economics of Energy

The Pros
and Cons
of Solar
Power

Laura L. Sullivan

Cavendish
Square

New York

Published in 2015 by Cavendish Square Publishing, LLC
243 5th Avenue, Suite 136, New York, NY 10016

Website: cavendishsq.com

This publication represents the opinions and views of the author based on his or her personal experience, knowledge, and
research. The information in this book serves as a general guide only. The author and publisher have used their best efforts in
preparing this book and disclaim liability rising directly or indirectly from the use and application of this book.

CPSIA Compliance Information: Batch #WS14CSQ

All websites were available and accurate when this book was sent to press.

Library of Congress Cataloging-in-Publication Data

Sullivan, Laura L. (Laura Lee), author.
The pros and cons of solar power / Laura L. Sullivan.
    pages cm. — (The economics of energy)
Includes bibliographical references and index.
ISBN 978-1-62712-924-4 (hardcover) ISBN 978-1-62712-926-8 (ebook)
1. Solar energy—Economic aspects—Juvenile literature. 2. Solar energy—Environmental aspects—Juvenile literature. I. Title.

TJ810.3.S85 2015
333.792'3—dc23

                    2014005316

ISBN 978-1-62712-924-4 (hardcover) ISBN 978-1-62712-926-8 (eBook)

Editorial Director: Dean Miller	Senior Book Designer: Amy Greenan
Editor: Kristen Susienka	Production Manager: Jennifer Ryder-Talbot
Senior Copy Editor: Wendy A. Reynolds	Production Editor: David McNamara
Art Director: Jeffrey Talbot	Photo Researcher: J8 Media

Printed in the United States of America

Table of Contents

Everything is Solar Powered

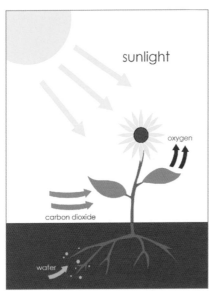

sunlight

oxygen

carbon dioxide

water

In a sense, the entire planet is solar powered. With the exception of certain types of Archaea that use inorganic matter like ammonia or sulfur, every life form on Earth depends either directly or indirectly on the sun for its energy and survival. Plants, cyanobacteria, and algae use **photosynthesis** to change sunlight into chemical **energy**. In the process, they produce their own carbohydrates and give off oxygen as a by-product. Animals get their energy either by eating plants and using the energy that their food obtained from the sun, or by eating other animals that have eaten plants. The sun powers almost every living thing on Earth.

However, in this day and age we have to power far more than just our own bodies. Power is used for everything from survival (climate control, water purification, cooking) to the sort of luxuries that are now

Solar power is a clean energy source that might one day be able to meet our planet's energy needs.

considered necessities in many countries (transportation, artificial light). For generations, we have depended on Earth-based, **non-renewable** fossil fuel resources such as natural gas, coal, and petroleum. But supplies of these energy sources are limited, and they come at great cost— financial, political, and environmental. People have been searching for alternative energy sources that are bountiful and clean. Some believe that solar energy may be a good choice as a supplemental or even replacement energy source. Others, however, think that solar energy is impractical on a large scale.

This book will examine the history of solar power use. It will then look at the pros and cons of collecting, converting, and using solar power. Finally, it will look to the future, at new breakthroughs that might alter the economics of energy forever.

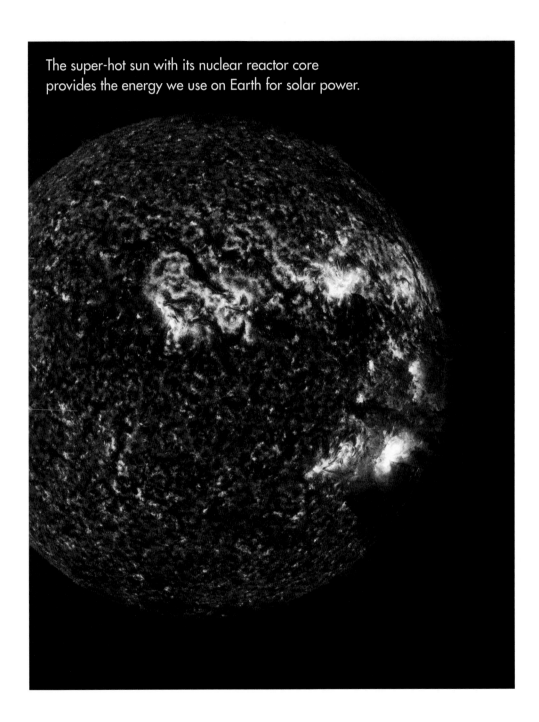

The super-hot sun with its nuclear reactor core
provides the energy we use on Earth for solar power.

Chapter 1

The History of Solar Power

What is the Sun?

To understand solar power, you must first understand the sun. The sun is a spherical ball of intertwined **plasma** and magnetic fields that is 109 times larger in diameter and 330,000 times more massive than Earth. In fact, the sun is so huge that it makes up 98 percent of all the matter in our solar system. That means the Earth, and all the planets, moons, and asteroids make up only 2 percent of the solar system. The sun is primarily composed of hydrogen and helium, with a little neon, oxygen, iron, and other elements.

About 4.6 billion years ago, a molecular cloud in space collapsed. The majority of the matter gathered in the center, where it became increasingly dense and hot until hydrogen atoms in the core began to collide. Thanks to these collisions, they joined to create new helium atoms and an amazing amount of energy in a process called **nuclear fusion**. (The leftover material from that initial collapse was flung outward and became the rest of our solar system.)

Ancient principles for passive solar homes are still applicable today, as seen in this modern building with southern exposure and overhangs.

The laws of physics in the sun are the same as they are on Earth—heat rises, and cold sinks. When the core of the sun is heated, gases begin to rise toward the exterior. This makes them cool slightly and sink toward the core again. There is always a circular motion of gases, called convection, within the sun. The surface of the sun is much cooler than the interior— only about 5,800 **kelvin**, as opposed to 15.7 million kelvin at the core. The surface of the sun has sunspots, which are darker, cooler areas of higher gravitational force. It also gives out solar flares, bursts of plasma and gas that can interfere with satellite communications on Earth, and cause the aurora borealis and aurora australis—the northern and southern lights. The sun emits several kinds of rays, including infrared, visible, and ultraviolet light, that reach the Earth's surface.

The Sun as a Power Source in Ancient Times

The sun has long been recognized as a source of awesome power, even when humans had no idea how to harness any of it. Nearly every culture around the globe worshipped some form of solar deity at one point in its history. They created mythologies to explain various solar phenomena, such as eclipses, and the seasonal disparity of daily hours of sunlight. Our earliest ancestors used the sun's energy in the most basic way, harvesting food during the hot season when plants grew abundantly, and storing the food (a kind of energy) during the time when the sun's rays were weakest. Some also used the sun to dry food for storage. Later, they developed much more sophisticated techniques for putting the sun to work for them.

Passive Solar Energy

Almost as soon as civilization evolved, people started taking advantage of the sun's properties in their building design. They used principles of **passive solar** heating (and cooling) whereby the position and materials of the house work to maximize (or minimize) warmth from the sun.

One of the earliest examples is found in ancient Greece. The famous Greek playwright Aeschylus (born about 525 BCE) wrote, "Only primitives and barbarians lack the knowledge of houses turned to face the winter

A DEEPER DIVE

Most Power is Solar Power

Do you think you know what solar energy is? Most people think of solar energy as harvesting light and converting it, by means of a photovoltaic cell or other mediums, into power. In reality, our planet has been converting solar energy into power for millions of years before humans existed. The most commonly used kinds of power (except nuclear, geothermal, and tidal hydropower) are ultimately derived from the sun.

Fossil fuels: Coal is formed by the decomposition and compression of dead vegetation over time. The energy that was in the vegetation's living tissue is changed into coal over millions of years. Where did the plants' energy originally come from? The sun. Similarly, petroleum and natural gas are formed from zooplankton (animals) and phytoplankton (plants) that when alive got their energy either directly or secondhand from the sun. Fossil fuels are solar energy that is millions of years old.

Hydropower: Hydropower uses the forceful movement of water to generate energy. Hydroelectric dams are the most common, but the power of ocean waves and currents can also be gathered. What does the sun have to do with water? The sun is responsible for the water cycle, the

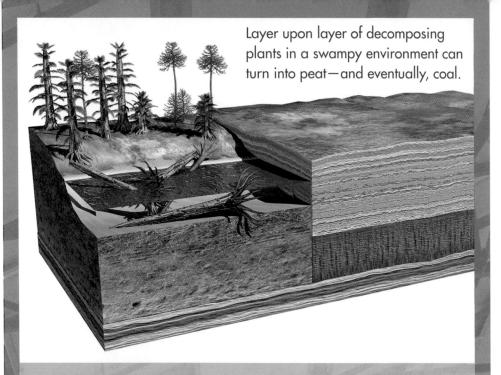

Layer upon layer of decomposing plants in a swampy environment can turn into peat—and eventually, coal.

process by which water evaporates, forms clouds, falls as rain, and repeats the process. This cycle keeps the world's oceans and rivers full.

Wind energy: When the sun warms Earth, it generates much of the planet's weather. Wind is caused by differences in atmospheric pressure. While some of this is simply from the Earth's rotation, a large factor is the difference in temperature between the equator and the poles, caused by the sun.

Biomass and biofuel: Biomass was mankind's earliest fuel. It usually refers to any plant that can be burned as fuel, like firewood, but some cultures use bones, animal fats, or dung as biomass fuel. Regardless, the origin of biomass energy is the sun. Today, biomass can also be converted into fuels such as biodiesel or bioethanol.

The Ancestral Pueblo peoples built the Cliff Palace (in Mesa Verde National Park, Colorado) to maximize solar potential.

sun." As Greek cities and city-states expanded, traditional fuels such as wood were exhausted, and residents had to think about other ways to heat their homes. Passive solar heat couldn't replace fuel fires in the coldest winters, but the designs maximized available heat and made living spaces much more comfortable.

Houses were built with southern exposure, and featured eaves and overhangs. During the summer when the sun was high in the sky, the overhangs would shade the house, blocking the light and heat and keeping the building cooler. In the winter, however, when the tilt of the

Earth made the path of the sun dip much farther to the south, the sun's rays would shine under the overhang, directly in the house, providing optimal warmth.

In North America, the Ancestral Pueblo peoples (frequently called the Anasazi) who lived in present-day Colorado and the surrounding regions also took advantage of passive solar construction. In the twelfth to thirteenth centuries CE, they built cliff dwellings under massive stone overhangs so that their ancient towns and cities kept cool in the summer, and received direct sunlight all through the winter. The Ancestral Pueblo people used another passive solar heating principle in conjunction with southern exposure—thermal mass. This means that dense building materials like stone are subject to less temperature fluctuation than wood and other less-dense materials. They carved their homes from thick sandstone, which held the night's coolness through the heat of the day in summer, and trapped the sun's heat to keep the buildings warmer through winter nights.

Other Ancient Uses of Solar Power

Ancient Rome, which adopted many Greek ideas, also made use of southern-facing dwellings. By the sixth century CE, the use of passive solar heat for homes was so pervasive that the Justinian Code—a set of laws written by the Byzantine Emperor Justinian—even included specific "sun rights" to ensure that neighbors never blocked each other's sunshine with new construction.

In the first century CE, author and orator Pliny the Younger had mica windows installed in one section of his northern Italian villa, because he found that they trapped heat during the day and gave it off at night,

A DEEPER DIVE

Could the Archimedes Solar Weapon Work?

Several hundred years after the fact, the author Lucien wrote that Archimedes used fire to destroy the enemy ships of the attacking Roman fleet during the Siege of Syracuse. Hundreds of years after that, another writer, Anthemius of Tralles, stated that Archimedes used "burning glasses," or what became known as the Archimedes heat ray. Was this a fact that trickled through history without further detail, or the invention of later authors eager for a good story?

Archimedes was a scientist and inventor who lived in Greece from 287 to 212 BCE. Though some historians suggest that he used a form of magnifying glass, most believe that if such a maneuver was actually attempted, a series of polished copper or bronze shields would have been used to act as **parabolic reflectors**, focusing the sunlight on one particular spot until it ignited. However, several modern experiments have shown that though the design had some merit, it probably wasn't practical. It would only be feasible if the target was motionless and if

For centuries, historians and scientists have debated whether Archimedes really used a solar heat ray against the attacking Roman fleet. This modern experiment to test the theory had mixed results.

no one from the crew took measures to stop the process, such as throwing water on the focal point to cool it down—neither of which is likely in battle conditions. The most convincing proof that Archimedes' weapon belongs in the realm of legend is that it was never apparently used again in warfare. Weapons that work are usually used repeatedly.

warming the chilly room. Romans wanted to grow the exotic foods they'd discovered in their far-flung empire, and constructed solar thermal-trapping hothouses to cultivate the most delicate crops even in cold weather.

There are stories that Greek, Roman, and Chinese civilizations would use mirrors or lenses to concentrate the sun's rays enough to light ceremonial flames for religious purposes. There is even a story that around 212 BCE, during the Siege of Syracuse, the inventor Archimedes developed a way to burn the invading fleet by arranging highly polished bronze shields to reflect and concentrate sunlight onto enemy ships. Though this might be no more than a myth, it is clear that later historians understood the concept of creating heat with concentrated sunlight.

The Enlightenment Looks to Sunlight

The Dark Ages really were dark when it came to solar power. Greek and Roman innovations about strategic solar building and use of glass were largely abandoned in Europe, though China continued its tradition of constructing southern-facing buildings. It wasn't until the Enlightenment that scientists began to rediscover the potential of solar power.

The Enlightenment was a movement in late seventeenth- and eighteenth-century Europe that promoted rationalism and science as a way to achieve reform. In 1633, Galileo was persecuted by the Catholic Church for declaring that the sun was in the center of the solar system. However, by the end of that century the scientific tide had turned and new ideas were being more readily accepted. In 1695, French scientist and author Georges-Louis Leclerc, Comte de Buffon, used mirrors to focus sunlight. He not only achieved a temperature hot enough to burn wood, but to melt lead as

France led the way in solar experimentation during the Enlightenment, with Georges-Louis Leclerc, Comte de Buffon, and Antoine Lavoisier (pictured here with his wife, chemist Marie-Anne Pierette Paulze) making great strides.

well. In 1782, his countryman Antoine Lavoisier managed to focus sunlight with a lens to achieve a temperature of 5,000 degrees Fahrenheit (2760 degrees Celsius)—hot enough to melt the previously unmeltable platinum.

In the seventeenth and eighteenth centuries, scientists were starting to put sunlight to other uses, too. In 1767, Swiss naturalist and physicist Horace-Bénédict de Saussure constructed the world's first documented solar oven. The well-insulated box he built had three layers of glass, and reached a cooking temperature of 230 degrees Fahrenheit (110 degrees Celsius). He experimented with the box at different altitudes and air temperatures, and found that the concentrated, trapped heat did not depend on any external factor but sunlight.

A DEEPER DIVE

An Eighteenth Century Hypothesis About Sunlight

Despite his experimental findings, Horace-Bénédict de Saussure didn't have a really accurate idea how his device worked, nor did he understand the nature of sunlight. He stated that: "Physicists are not unanimous as to the nature of sunlight. Some regard it as the same element as fire, but in its greatest purity. Others envisage it as an entity with a nature completely different from fire, and which, incapable of itself heating, has only the power to give an igneous fluid the movement which produces heat."

Still, his experiments were valid, and he understood the potential of sunlight as a power source, if not sunlight's exact nature.

Solar Saltations in the Nineteenth Century

Before the nineteenth century, putting the sun to use meant simply capturing its heat through the use of mirrors, lenses, absorption, and insulation. In 1839, for the first time, someone discovered how to turn the sun's light into electrical power. French scientist Alexandre-Edmond Becquerel was only nineteen when, while experimenting in his father's laboratory, he discovered the **photovoltaic effect**. He connected platinum electrodes to silver chloride in an acidic solution, and exposed it all to sunlight. He found that this could produce a weak electric current. He had discovered the principle that is used for some of the most advanced solar technology today.

Becquerel made the photovoltaic discovery, but he couldn't put it to practical use. French inventor Augustin Mouchot returned to the origins of solar science by using sunlight simply as a concentrated heat source. Then, he took it one step further and found a way to convert the heat to mechanical output by rigging a solar steam engine.

Concern over dependence on rapidly disappearing non-renewable energy isn't just a modern occurrence. In the nineteenth century, Mouchot feared that the rapid expansion of the Industrial Revolution in Europe could be brought to a screeching halt if coal supplies ran out. "Eventually industry will no longer find in Europe the resources to satisfy its prodigious expansion," Mouchot said after a demonstration of one of his solar engines. "Coal will undoubtedly be used up. What will industry do then?" He was dedicated to the idea of finding a new, renewable energy source. After much study and experimentation, he believed that solar power would provide the answer for the future of industrialization.

A DEEPER DIVE

The Photovoltaic Effect

The photovoltaic effect is the process by which a material exposed to light (sunlight or other light) produces an electrical current. This happens at the atomic level. Certain materials will absorb photons from light and release **electrons**. When the free electrons are captured, voltage is generated.

A solar cell, or photovoltaic cell, is made from **semiconductors** such as silicon. (A semiconductor can conduct electricity, just not as well as metals. Thus, the electricity that passes through it can be more easily managed and captured.) There are two layers of semiconductor, which are each formulated to have slightly different properties. When the semiconductors' atoms are bombarded with light, electrons are knocked loose. They can move from one layer into the other, but not back again. This imbalance creates an excess of energy. When electrical conductors are attached to the positive and the negative sides, the electrons can be harnessed in the form of an electrical current.

Augustin Mouchot devised a solar powered steam engine in nineteenth century France. This engine was used to power a printing press.

Mouchot first experimented with solar cooking, and then applied what he'd learned in that field to making solar engines. He used concentrated solar thermal power to boil water, and used the resulting steam to power an engine. His invention impressed Emperor Napoleon III, who provided the funding for Mouchot to continue building bigger and more powerful solar steam engines. He set up solar engines in sunny Algeria, and later won an award for using solar heat to make ice.

The government put Mouchot's dreams of renewable energy on the back burner, however, when the dwindling coal supply was suddenly buttressed by both a free trade treaty with the United Kingdom (UK) and improved methods of coal transportation. Coal was suddenly cheap, and there was no pressing need for an alternative. Europe would continue to rely on coal to power its industry.

Harness the Sun at Home: Solar Snacks

You can use the sun to cook your own food. A solar cooker (or solar oven) is a way to heat and even cook many kinds of food using only heat generated by the sun. Solar cookers work by concentrating sunlight with the use of reflective surfaces, such as mirrors or shiny foil, using a low-reflective interior to convert the light to heat, and then trapping the heat inside the cooker.

It is simple to make one using materials you probably already have around the house.

*Safety First! Have an adult help you with the cutting, and make sure to use oven mitts when handling hot food.

A Basic Solar Cooker

You will need:
One cardboard box (A pizza box or a shoe box will work.)
Aluminum foil
Clear plastic wrap
Black paper
Glue and/or tape
Scissors or box cutter
Pencil or marker
Ruler
A stick (Your ruler or pencil can double for the stick.)

First, apply glue to the sides of the inside of the box (not the bottom) and attach aluminum foil. Make sure the shiny side is facing outward, and keep the foil as smooth as possible. The foil will reflect and concentrate the sunlight. Then, glue black paper to the bottom. Black absorbs light and converts it to heat.

Put the lid on the box, and use your ruler to trace a square or rectangle with the edges about an inch away from the edges of the box. Using scissors or a box cutter, cut THREE SIDES ONLY. If you are using a shoe box, leave one of the longer sides of the rectangle intact. If you are using a pizza box, leave the hinge side uncut. Next, glue aluminum foil, shiny side out, to the bottom of the flap you just cut.

Lift the flap and stretch clear plastic wrap over the opening. (The lid should be closed but the flap open.) Tape the plastic down on the sides, making sure you can still open and close the box.

Place the oven outside in full sunlight on a warm day. The sky should be clear and the temperature at least 60 degrees Fahrenheit (15.5 degrees Celsius), preferably more. Put the food you'll be cooking on a separate piece of aluminum foil, a paper plate or an oven-safe dish, and place it in the center of the black paper. Prop the flap up so it is slightly angled toward the food.

Solar S'mores

You will need:
Marshmallows
Graham crackers
Chocolate (thin squares or bars)
Aluminum foil or paper plate

Make a solar cooker as above. Separate four graham crackers into eight squares, and place a marshmallow on four of the halves. Put them on aluminum foil or a paper plate, and set them in the middle of the black paper on the bottom of your solar cooker. After 30–40 minutes the marshmallows should get soft. Open the lid, and put one chocolate square and another graham cracker half on top of the marshmallow. Press each one down, close the oven, and leave them inside for another five minutes until the chocolate starts to melt.

These thermodynamic panels on a house in Belgium are a more modern take on the rooftop solar water heaters that Clarence Kemp popularized in the late nineteenth century.

Solar Power Goes Commercial

Clarence Kemp was a man of little formal education but a genius for invention. He founded the C.M. Kemp Manufacturing Company in 1881, and then in 1891 put the first commercially viable solar water heater into production. He is considered the father of solar energy in the United States.

Previously, homes in the nineteenth century generally heated household water using a wood or coal stove. A coiled pipe carried water through the stove, heating it and shunting it where it was needed in the house.

In cold weather this wasn't a problem, as the stove would be lit most of the time. But in hot weather—and particularly in hot climates—this was inconvenient and uncomfortable. People wanted a hot bath without heating up the entire house.

In 1895, Kemp sold exclusive manufacturing rights to two California businessmen. Before long, about 30 percent of homes in Pasadena, California, were using Kemp's patented Climax solar water heating system. The invention consisted of three tanks in an insulating frame, with a glass surface facing the south side of the house. Though it promised to give hot water all day and night, it was really only effective in the afternoon and evening. It was named Climax for the way the water temperature increased throughout the morning, reaching its hottest level later in the day. Consumers could purchase a solar water heater for $25, and expect to save about $9 each year in fuel costs.

The Twentieth Century

Solar power made its next great leap at Bell Laboratories. Three scientists—Daryl Chapin, Gerald Pearson, and Calvin Fuller—came up with a photovoltaic cell capable of delivering a significantly greater current. Their major breakthrough was to use silicon rather than selenium as a semiconductor. The new cell had a 6 percent efficiency rate, which was five times greater than the most efficient selenium cell.

Bell Laboratories was so excited about the discovery that they held a press conference to show off the invention. On the front page of its April 26, 1954 edition, the *New York Times* declared that this was "the beginning of a new era, leading eventually to the realization of one of

A DEEPER DIVE

The Oil Crisis Brought Change—Good and Bad

The 1973 Oil Crisis had the positive effect of forcing people to consider alternative energy, including renewable sources such as wind and solar energy. However, it had negative consequences, too, even beyond the economic impact of limited and expensive oil.

The crisis made the United States focus on exploiting local oil sources. Though the country has dramatically reduced its dependence on foreign oil, the environmental consequences have been considerable. Pipelines damage sensitive tundra and permafrost landscapes in Alaska. Fracking is having an impact on things from groundwater to seismic activity. Oil platform disasters in the Gulf of Mexico, such as the *Deepwater Horizon* explosion and spill of 2010, have wreaked havoc on marine ecosystems. Other non-renewable alternative energy sources have also come to the fore, each with its own risks. Coal mining in the Appalachian Mountains is often done by a technique known as mountaintop removal mining, which not only

During the Oil Crisis of 1973, many U.S. service stations ran out of gasoline.

affects local biodiversity but adds toxins to the watersheds and air, leading to serious human health concerns. The United States also increased its dependence on nuclear power. Nuclear facilities generate radioactive waste that can remain hazardous for generations, and any accident, terrorist attack, or malfunction at a nuclear power plant could be catastrophic.

Oil can harm the environment at all stages of its use. The devastation caused by the explosion of the *Deepwater Horizon* oil rig in 2010 will be felt in the environment for decades.

mankind's most cherished dreams—the harnessing of the almost limitless energy of the sun for the uses of civilization."

The Oil Crisis of 1973 provided the greatest twentieth-century incentive to find alternative sources of energy. At that time, the Organization of Arab Petroleum Exporting Countries (OAPEC) declared an oil embargo. From October 1973 to March 1974, the oil-producing Arab countries raised the price of crude oil by 70 percent, and dramatically reduced their output. Since the United States and other industrialized economies depended on petroleum products, and OAPEC was the primary supplier, this caused panic and economic instability. People started to seriously think about ways to minimize their reliance on foreign oil. A popular suggestion was to turn to **renewable resources**, including solar power.

CRITICAL THINKING

- How does the sun influence life on Earth? How might the planet be different if it was a little closer, or farther away, from the sun?

- Why do you think the sun was often considered a god or goddess in ancient times? How did the sun influence people's lives even before they understood the science of the sun? Do you know of any myths that help explain aspects of the sun? (Hint: The myth of Persephone is one example.)

- Consider your own house, or buildings in your city. Are any of them designed taking the sun into consideration? Which way do windows face? Where are trees planted? What are the buildings made from? How might these things contribute to passive solar heating in your area?

- The Oil Crisis of 1973 made people start to think about alternative energy. Do you think fear is a great motivator for science and technology? What is happening today that might scare people into seeking new discoveries?

Insolation, a measure of how much solar radiation strikes a surface, varies by location and season.

Chapter 2

The Pros of Solar Power

There are many advantages to using solar power. Some people believe that because of the advantages, it should one day be mankind's primary power source.

Sunlight is Abundant

For an energy source to be practical it must be abundant—and there is plenty of sunshine to go around.

The sun is a giant nuclear reactor, which produces energy by the process of nuclear fusion in its core. In the sun's nuclear fusion, hydrogen atoms collide at high rates of speed and produce helium. Unlike most reactions, matter is not conserved. Rather, some of the mass from the hydrogen nuclei is changed into energy in the form of **photons**. (This is opposed to the nuclear reaction that takes place in man-made power plants. That is **nuclear fission**, where an atom's nucleus splits, releasing energy.) The sun fuses 620 million metric tons of hydrogen in its core every second.

The sun will be a reliable source of energy for at least another four billion years.

After energy forms in the sun's core, it takes a long time for it to reach the surface and be cast out into the universe. Depending on conditions, it can take as few as 10,000 years to as many as 170,000 years for the energy to reach the sun's exterior and escape in the form of light.

The sun produces and emits many kinds of electromagnetic radiation. It makes Gamma rays, which are extremely high-energy and very dangerous to biological life. Luckily, these rays are changed into a lower-energy form before they exit the sun. The sun also produces ultraviolet light, infrared light, X-rays, visible light, and radio waves. Of these, infrared, visible, and ultraviolet light reach the Earth's surface. At the outer edge of our atmosphere, the composition is about 50 percent infrared, 40 percent visible, and 10 percent ultraviolet. After passing through Earth's atmosphere, the ratio is about 44 percent visible light, a maximum of 3 percent ultraviolet when the sun is at its highest, and the rest is infrared.

The sun is about 93 million miles from Earth, and it takes sunlight a little over eight minutes to reach our planet. **Insolation** is the measure of how much solar energy reaches the ground at any given time. Some solar energy is reflected back into space by Earth's atmosphere, but on average every square meter of ground receives about 445 watts of visible light energy, 527 watts of infrared, and 32 watts of ultraviolet light when the sun is at its zenith. In total, the Earth absorbs about 3,850,000 **exajoules** of energy each year. (A single **joule** is the energy required to produce one watt of power for one second. An exajoule is 1,000,000,000,000,000,000 joules.) This means that the sun gives Earth more energy in one hour than humans use in a year. The amount of solar energy that reaches Earth in one year is more than the total cumulative energy available from all non-renewable energy sources (like coal, oil, uranium, gas) past, present, and future.

Solar Energy is Renewable

The major problem with most of the things we use for fuel is that they will eventually run out. Technically, oil, gas, and coal are still forming—plants and microorganisms are still dying and being converted under pressure—but this process can take millions of years. Sources don't agree on how long known supplies of coal and petroleum will last, but few of the estimates are more than several hundred years. It simply isn't feasible to wait for the Earth's natural processes to produce more of these resources.

Solar energy, however, is renewable for at least as long as life on Earth exists. Every day, without fail, the sun will rise—at least for the next few billion years.

The sun has been fairly stable in its processes for about four billion years, and will probably remain stable for at least four billion more. Eventually, the nuclear fusion of hydrogen into helium that takes place in its core will cease, and the sun will begin transformations that will lead to its demise. But until then, we have an abundance of sunlight to work with.

Solar Power is Sustainable

When people talk about energy policy, they often use the word sustainable. Many think that 'sustainable' is synonymous with 'renewable,' but the concept is farther reaching. Sustainable energy doesn't just look to the future of the resource, but also to the future of the people who use it. It takes into account the idea that perhaps people should not have current benefits at great future costs. The UK's Renewable Energy and Efficiency Partnership defines sustainability as, "Effectively, the provision of energy such that it meets the needs of the present without compromising the ability of future generations to meet their own needs ... Sustainable energy has two key components: renewable energy, and energy efficiency."

As noted above, solar energy is for all practical purposes renewable for the foreseeable life of the human species. It is also a form of energy that has very little negative environmental impact. Coal, petroleum, and nuclear energies all have great environmental costs that have already been detrimental to our health and well-being. Global warming is the result not just of current energy policies, but those of our forebears. The

Large-scale solar plants, like this one in France, can harness energy for the **grid** in a sustainable, clean way.

energy choices we make now will affect the world our children will live in.

Solar energy can also be a part of industrial sustainability. Currently, factories and infrastructure are generally built as if there will be no end of coal and petroleum—yet when the supplies do end, the entire global economic structure will have to be altered. If solar power is put into use now, though technologies might drastically improve, the basic method of energy collection and use can be constant through the generations.

The Cost of Solar is Dropping

One of the longstanding arguments against solar power has been its cost. While the startup costs of utilizing solar power are still high, the price is

A DEEPER DIVE

The Greenhouse Effect and Global Warming

Think of a greenhouse for plants. It works by collecting light and heat from the sun, and reflecting it back inside the building to increase the temperature. A similar principle applies, on a larger scale, to our planet in the **greenhouse effect**. Solar radiation passes through the atmosphere (though some is reflected back into space) and warms the Earth. A portion of the thermal radiation coming off the Earth is then radiated back up to the greenhouse gases in the atmosphere. These gases absorb and then bounce back the thermal radiation in all directions. Some of it is sent back to Earth, increasing the temperature.

The greenhouse effect is not in itself a bad thing—in fact, it makes life as we know it possible on Earth, by trapping enough heat to sustain life. But anthropogenic (human-created) activity has increased the amount of greenhouse gases in the atmosphere, heightening the greenhouse effect and increasing the average global temperature.

Several gases—as well as clouds—are involved in the greenhouse effect, including carbon dioxide, water vapor, methane, and ozone. Carbon dioxide, which is produced primarily by fossil fuel combustion, is considered the worst culprit in global warming.

In the last century, air and sea temperatures on Earth have increased by about 1.4 degrees Fahrenheit (0.8 degrees Celsius). Our planet has been warming faster and faster—two-thirds of that increase has occurred since 1980. The Intergovernmental Panel on Climate Change offered its projections on climate change in 2007. It calculated that, at the most hopeful end of their emissions estimates, the global temperature would rise 2.0 to 5.2 degrees Fahrenheit (1.1 to 2.9 degrees Celsius) during the twenty-first century. At the grimmer end of their predictions, it calculated that temperatures might rise as much as 4.3 to 11.5 degrees Fahrenheit (2.4 to 6.4 degrees Celsius).

Though some question whether human activity is really responsible for the growing climate shift, in 2013 the IPCC said that, "Human influence has been detected in warming of the atmosphere and ocean, in changes in the global water cycle, in reductions in snow and ice, in global mean sea level rise, and in changes in some climate extremes. This evidence for human influence has grown since (the 2007 assessment). It is extremely likely (95 to 100 percent) that human influence has been the dominant cause of the observed warming since the mid-twentieth century."

Homeowners can get tax breaks and rebates when they install rooftop solar panels to generate electricity.

coming down. Installation is usually the only cost—there is little to no system maintenance required. As of 2011, the per-watt cost of existing solar power technology dropped lower than the cost of nuclear power, and the price is estimated to keep falling.

Furthermore, those who use solar power are reaping some financial rewards. Homeowners who have set up solar panels on their homes can either use the energy they collect to meet the needs of their own homes, or sell the power back to the grid. In either case, the savings eventually add up to offset the initial cost of installation. For example, according to Europe's Energy Portal (www.energy.eu), using 2012 data, if the energy cost in Italy is 0.20 euros per **kilowatt hour (kWh)** and the local insolation is 1350 kWh per kilowatt peak (kWp), the homeowner saves 270 euros per year, and recoups the installation cost in about seven years.

In the United States and elsewhere, federal, state, and local governments offer money back to consumers to encourage people to use solar energy. In the U.S., 30 percent of solar installation costs can be deducted from federal income taxes. As part of the California Solar Initiative, residents of that state can receive additional incentives which, when combined with federal programs, can cut the cost of installing solar power systems by 50 percent.

Solar is Environmentally Friendly

Solar power has very little negative effect on the environment—which makes it a valuable energy source in a world that has been drastically altered by the use of fossil fuels.

The fuels that dominate today are harmful to the environment. According to the Environmental Protection Agency (EPA), the power sources that humans rely on for the bulk of their energy needs—petroleum, coal, and other fossil fuels—were responsible for 79 percent of greenhouse gas production in the U.S. Coal mining damages the environment with destruction of habitat and water pollution. After it is mined, coal is burned to generate electricity in power plants, producing 42 percent of the U.S. electrical supply in 2011. The combustion releases hazardous chemicals into the atmosphere. Petroleum products are mostly

An accident when extracting or transporting fossil fuels can cause collateral damage. This oil-covered brown pelican in Barataria Bay near Grand Isle, Louisiana, was one of the victims of the 2010 BP oil spill.

used in vehicles. Environmental damage is caused during oil extraction, transportation, from oil spills, and from the particulates generated during its combustion.

The EPA says that unless annual emissions of greenhouse gases significantly decrease, the concentration of those gases in the Earth's atmosphere will increase, leading to:

- Elevation of the average global temperature
- Altered weather patterns, including amounts of rain and snow
- Reduction of polar ice, snow, and permafrost
- Raised sea levels
- Increased ocean acidity

These changes will affect the planet's livability. They will have a negative impact on ecosystems, water and food supplies, and human health.

Solar is one of the cleanest energy sources. In itself, it produces no hazardous emissions. In 2011, the Intergovernmental Panel on Climate Change (IPCC) collected data on the total life cycle of greenhouse gas emissions for all major power sources. It looked at all the possible greenhouse gas production (mostly carbon dioxide) over every step of obtaining the fuel, manufacturing components to use it, transportation, maintenance, and disposal. The panel found that solar energy produced 22–46 grams per kilowatt hour (g/kWh), depending on whether photovoltaic or solar thermal methods were used. In comparison, a coal-fired power plant produced 915–994 g/kWh.

Solar is Versatile for Many Applications

Today, solar technology has advanced to the point where the sun can be used to power many things. Solar energy is used in applications ranging from the very small, such as personal calculators or landscaping lights, to entire houses existing off-grid, with all their energy needs met entirely by solar power. Now that the cost of solar energy is falling, it is even being used to power the grid itself.

There are two main ways to collect power from the sun: photovoltaics, and **concentrated solar power (CSP)**. As previously described, photovoltaics uses two layers of slightly different semiconductors which, when exposed to light, release free electrons that can be collected in a current. CSP uses the same principle as the earliest solar cookers, and even Archimedes' legendary heat ray—concentrating solar thermal energy

Solar power plants such as this concentrated solar power (CSP) facility in Spain generate no greenhouse gases—the only pollution comes from manufacturing the equipment for the plant.

into a small area and using the heat to make steam, which is used to produce electricity. There are many modern applications of both kinds of solar power.

Small Consumer Goods

Solar power has entered the home—even indoors, where the sun might only shine through windows, or not at all. Solar-powered calculators, invented in the 1970s, are a mainstay of modern math classes. They have tiny photovoltaic cells that use ambient light from windows or electric lights for

Solar power has entered our homes and gardens with ubiquitous and inexpensive photovoltaic outdoor lighting.

power. Another use of photovoltaics that has taken off is in outdoor lighting. Few landscaped yards now have cords running underground to power footlights and garden lights. The majority of available outdoor lighting options are now solar-powered, mass-produced, and inexpensive.

Water Heating

Ever since Kemp's Climax solar water heater was patented, methods for using the sun to provide hot household water have been improving. In locations between 40 degrees north latitude and 40 degrees south latitude, solar power is capable of providing up to 70 percent of a home's hot water, at temperatures up to 140 degrees Fahrenheit (60 degrees Celsius). Many swimming pools are also heated with solar power.

Home Heating and Cooling

Homes and other buildings can be heated—and even cooled—with solar energy. Heating is relatively straightforward, with air being warmed by

Solar water heating is one of the most popular applications of solar energy in the United States and in the world, as seen here on this South African rooftop.

means of an absorbing medium that captures the sun's heat.

Solar cooling is more expensive than heating, and is more appropriate for industry than private home use. The process uses solar heat to change a substance from a liquid to a gas, and then force the gas into an area of lower pressure. The low pressure forces the gas to have a lower temperature. This lower-temperature gas then absorbs unwanted heat from the area to be cooled, and is forced into a high-pressure chamber, where the excess heat is disbursed outside the building.

Power for the Grid

Both photovoltaics and CSP can be used to provide energy for power plants to deliver to homes, just as a fossil fuel-burning power plant can. Massive arrays of solar cells are arranged to maximize light collection in 'solar farms.' As of 2013, the global output of photovoltaic power plants is 12 gigawatts. CSP systems not only concentrate the sunlight, they also track it throughout the day to maximize efficiency. There are several main kinds of CSP collectors—the parabolic trough, enclosed trough, Fresnel reflectors, dish Stirling engine systems, and solar power towers. The efficiency of CSP systems is increasing, and

The Tokai Challenger won the 2009 Global Green Challenge race in Australia for solar cars. It had an average speed of 100.5 kilometers per hour.

the cost is declining. The Ivanpah Solar Power Facility, currently under construction in California's Mojave Desert, is projected to provide power more cheaply than photovoltaic power, and at about the same cost as natural gas.

Transportation

Directly solar-charged vehicles—such as cars fueled entirely by photovoltaic cells on their roofs—might not be practical yet, but many vehicles are already running off of indirect solar power. Some electric vehicles have a solar-powered charging system. Some researchers think that the future of solar technology lies not in using the sun to produce electricity, but rather using it to produce hydrogen. Soon, cars might be powered by hydrogen produced through solar means.

The NASA Pathfinder is an unmanned solar airplane that NASA hopes will lead to high-altitude planes that can perform long-term missions for communications and atmospheric study.

Solar-powered planes, both manned and unmanned, are taking to the skies, and solar boats have circumnavigated the globe. Solar power is particularly suitable for large, slow-moving vessels. Solar energy is even used for power and propulsion in space.

Solar is Silent and Still

Another popular renewable and non-polluting energy source is wind power. Wind turbines are essentially advanced windmills that turn the kinetic energy produced by the wind into electrical energy. However, they produce low-frequency vibrations, which some people claim cause intense annoyance, and physiological symptoms such as nausea, vertigo, and insomnia—a collection of reactions called "wind turbine syndrome." Though studies cast doubt on the actual effect of wind turbines on humans, there is no doubt that they have a devastating local effect on bird and bat populations, killing thousands, even hundreds of thousands, each year. Solar power production is silent, causing no physiological symptoms in humans. What's more, it has no or few moving parts, and does not contribute to traumatic bird or bat deaths.

Wind turbines contribute to bird and bat deaths, and are thought by some to produce a "wind turbine syndrome" effect in humans with the low frequency sounds they produce.

Solar Components are Low Maintenance

Solar power systems rarely require maintenance. Once they are installed, most reliable companies offer warranties of around twenty-five years on solar cells. The photovoltaic panels require no maintenance beyond making sure that leaves or other debris don't cover them and block out the sun. Solar water heating systems need to be checked periodically for corrosion or scaling, but should last at least as long as photovoltaic panels.

Technology is Rapidly Improving

With the need for alternative, clean, renewable energies so pressing, some governments and corporations provide incentives for scientists and amateurs to develop new solar technologies. One such program is the biennial World Solar Challenge, during which competitors race solar-powered cars across the Australian continent. Each race sees new improvements in the cars.

Solar panels are becoming cheaper and more efficient, for homes and for utility-level power for the grid. Nanotechnology—making and using matter at its very smallest size, down to one-billionth of a meter—is contributing to the development of solar cells made from graphene, an inexpensive and nontoxic substance. A new class of crystalline materials called perovskites is also showing promise for use in high-efficiency solar cells. One day, the cost of solar energy around the world might be on par with that of fossil fuels—with far less collateral damage to our present, and far more sustainability for our future.

CRITICAL THINKING

- Will there ever come a time when all of mankind's energy needs are met by the sun? What would have to change to make this possible?

- How do you picture the future of Earth? Are you optimistic about being able to stop global warming? What clues from history or human nature shape your answer?

- Should cost be a consideration if human health and the future of the planet and environment are at stake? How do we balance the needs of today with those of generations to come?

- Think about the tradeoff between fossil fuel use and the environment. In what ways might the ecological damage be worth the benefits that fossil fuels have given society? How would the planet be different—for better or for worse—if we had never used fossil fuels, only solar power?

- What other applications might there be for solar energy? Can you think of everyday things that could be run on solar power? What about entirely new technology—what solar invention would you create?

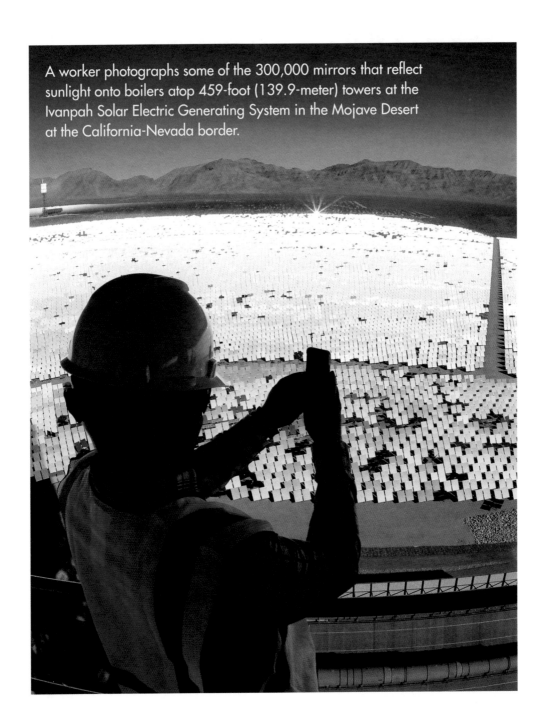

A worker photographs some of the 300,000 mirrors that reflect sunlight onto boilers atop 459-foot (139.9-meter) towers at the Ivanpah Solar Electric Generating System in the Mojave Desert at the California-Nevada border.

Chapter 3

The Cons of Solar Power

Despite its promise of providing clean energy, solar power has some drawbacks. Some people believe that they are severe enough to prevent solar energy from ever being our planet's dominant power source.

Solar Power is Still Too Expensive

The relative cost of solar power is debatable, and the price is getting lower all the time. Still, solar power is generally more costly than energy generated from fossil fuels. The Solar-Estimate website (www.find-solar.org), a not-for-profit project of SolarReviews.com, allows users to enter their location and current energy use to receive an estimate for the cost of solar power panel installation. In an example using the author's two-bedroom Florida home, a 5.35 kW system generating 7,385 kWh annually would cost approximately $20,422 in 2013. However, with combined tax credits and a considerable rebate from the author's local power company, the total out-of-pocket cost would be $6,792. According to the website, the money spent to install the system would be returned in energy savings in 4.72 years.

This combined cycle thermodynamic solar plant in Italy uses a tank of molten salt to store energy.

The Pros and Cons of Solar Power

In 2013, the U.S. Department of Energy's Energy Information Administration presented their analysis of the projected **levelized costs** of all forms of energy for power plants coming into service in 2018. The total system levelized cost (using 2011 U.S. dollar values) of a photovoltaic solar plant is $144.30 per **megawatt hour (mWh)**. For a solar thermal (CSP) plant, the cost is $261.5 per mWh produced. By contrast, a conventional coal plant is estimated to cost $100.10 per mWh, an advanced nuclear plant $89.6 per mWh, and a biomass plant $111 per mWh. The only kind of power plant expected to be more costly than solar in 2018 is an offshore wind power system.

Intermittent Availability

Solar (like wind) is considered an intermittent energy source because it is variable, both in time of day, and from day to day. According to the George Washington University Solar Institute, on a cloudless day at noon the average amount of sunlight hitting the Earth is 1,000 watts per square meter. However, this varies greatly depending on the location. An arid area with little cloud cover, such as a desert, might

The Finsterwalde Solar Power Plant in Germany is one of the largest solar installations in the world.

receive as much as 6 kWh per square meter per day, while a northern location such as Boston might only get 3.6 kWh per square meter per day. Time of year also makes a significant difference, with much less sunlight available in the winter as opposed to the summer. For example, an area like Seattle, Washington might get as little as 0.7 kWh per square meter per day during the winter. Solar power could not currently be a primary power source in all places, at all times of year.

Storage Problems

Although energy consumption tends to conveniently peak during the daylight hours when solar energy is readily available, power also has to be there for nighttime and cloudy days. Power plants have to be able to balance supply and demand all the time. Thus, energy derived from the sun has to be stored for future use. Utility-level CSP systems can sometimes store energy in the form of heat in tanks of molten salt.

But possibly the best solution—storing energy in batteries—is still far from perfect. The cost is still very high. Lithium-ion battery packs can cost around $1,000 per kWh. Though the cost is coming down thanks to research and development in the electric vehicle industry, storage of solar energy is still a major obstacle to its widespread grid use.

Ecological Impact and Pollution Associated with Solar Energy

Few things can be manufactured without some environmental cost, and the equipment associated with solar power is no exception. Though solar energy is clean, the construction of photovoltaic cells has been associated with emissions of the greenhouse gases nitrogen trifluoride and sulfur hexafluoride.

Another problem with solar power is that it requires vast amounts of land. The George Washington University Solar Institute calculated how much land would have to be used to provide all the energy needed to run the United States through photovoltaic cells. They came up with

The Les Mées solar power plant in southern France, with solar panels on rolling hills producing 36 megawatts, is one of the largest in that country.

0.7 percent of the U.S. landmass, or approximately 25,700 square miles (41,360 square kilometers). Covering such an area with photovoltaic cells (or CSP collectors) could harm delicate ecosystems and lead to habitat loss. While the effect can be mitigated by choosing low-quality land such as abandoned mining areas or reclaimed industrial zones, solar collecting still disrupts vast swaths of land, particularly if the site must be cleared and leveled, as is often necessary.

CRITICAL THINKING

- What are some ways of getting around the problem of intermittent light from the sun? What about storage, or combining solar power with another energy technology? What are the benefits and drawbacks of these solutions?

- Can anything be produced without some pollution or greenhouse gas emission? Look at some of the objects around you right now, and figure out where pollution might have been created along the path of their production and use.

Solar panels can bring electricity to the most remote regions. In this village in India, the residents say they mostly use electricity to power their cell phones.

Chapter 4

The Future of Solar Power

Some analysts believe that the future of solar power lies in developing nations. Many of the poorest countries, with residents living most remotely from established power grids, are in arid areas at low latitudes, and thus receive some of the most reliable supplies of solar energy. Many countries in Africa, for example, receive an average of 325 days of intense sunlight every year. They are ideally suited to take advantage of solar power at the village level, or even at the individual level.

Solar energy has the potential to improve health by providing clean water and alternatives to hazardous biofuel cooking. It can even improve the standard of living by supplementing education. Solar powered light enables students to do basic things, like studying at night, which many people in the industrialized parts of the world take for granted.

Small-Scale Electricity in Remote Locations

Currently, more than a billion people in the world have no electricity whatsoever. Sometimes it isn't feasible to connect remote locations to power grids. For those living in inaccessible areas, renewable power like solar can make the difference between having light after dark, heat in the cold weather, and even an Internet connection to the rest of the globe.

In many developing nations, the most common fuel source for light is kerosene. Consequently, lighting homes in the poorest regions costs much more than it does in the wealthiest nations. By converting to solar power for electrical needs, families' limited resources can be redirected to food or education. Kenya has made great strides in the use of solar power. About 30,000 small solar panels are sold in that country each year, mostly for use in rural communities. In fact, Kenya has the highest per capita use of solar systems of any country in the world. Each solar panel is capable of generating 12 to 30 watts. Some countries are expanding use of solar power on their own, while some are getting outside help. The Clean Development Mechanism program of the **Kyoto Protocol** provides a way for industrialized nations to invest in clean fuel alternatives for developing nations.

Safe Water from the Sun

One of the most serious threats to human health in developing nations is the lack of safe drinking water. Solar power can help solve this problem in several ways.

Solar power can be used to pump water from underground. Though the cost of a solar-powered pump is higher than other kinds of pumps, the system is virtually maintenance-free, and no additional fuel is required.

After that, there are several techniques—both high-tech and low-tech—to purify the water. On the high-tech end, for example, is a

Water-borne pathogens can be killed in a simple and inexpensive way using solar radiation and heat. This woman is placing water bottles on the roof of her home in the impoverished Kibera neighborhood of Nairobi to make clean drinking water for her family.

water purification facility in a community in the dense jungles of the Yucatan Peninsula in Mexico. The region is a day's drive from the closest source of safe, potable water. Researchers from the Massachusetts Institute of Technology have installed a solar-powered purification system. First, it uses solar-produced electricity to pump brackish, undrinkable water from underground. Then the solar electricity powers a reverse osmosis system, where the water is forced through semipermeable membranes to remove impurities, such as hazardous chemicals. The system produces 1,000 liters (264 gallons) of clean drinking water—even on a cloudy day. That is enough for the 450 residents of the remote village.

On the low-tech end, solar power can be used to boil water to kill pathogens. Alternatively, a method that has grown in popularity is SODIS—solar disinfection using the sun's ultraviolet light. Ultraviolet (UV) light is one of the types of light the sun gives off. It has a shorter wavelength than visible light, and cannot be seen by the human eye. There are several kinds of UV light with different wavelengths, including the UV-A and UV-B often mentioned on sunscreen labels. In this extremely simple system, water contaminated with disease-causing organisms like protists, bacteria, or worms, is placed in PET plastic bottles and exposed to direct sunlight for five to six hours. The sunlight kills pathogens in three ways. First, the long-wave UV-A light directly kills the bacteria. Secondly, the UV-A rays react with oxygen in the water to create free radicals that kill pathogens. Finally, the increased temperature inside the bottles kills harmful organisms. The high temperature even acts in synergy with the UV-A effects, speeding the process as temperatures rise.

Solar cookers can be used in developing countries as alternatives to biomass fuels, which can cause serious health problems.

Solar Ovens for Developing Nations

Because solar cookers are low-tech, easy to make and use, and require only basic materials, they are becoming increasingly popular in developing nations, particularly those near the equator where sunlight is abundant. Solar ovens use no fuel other than sunlight, and thus cost nothing to operate.

Traditionally, people in developing nations cooked using biomass fuels such as wood, dung, and charcoal. When these substances burn, they give off smoke, particles, and poisonous gases that can lead to lung and eye diseases. Since the biomass cooking often happens inside, women and children in particular can be subjected to many hours of harmful inhalants every day. A study estimated that in 2000, between 1.5 and 2 million deaths in developing nations were caused by indoor air pollution, primarily from biomass fuel combustion.

Solar cookers, however, present none of these problems. A solar cooker can reach temperatures of 325 degrees Fahrenheit (163 degrees Celsius), which can cook foods as well as sterilize or pasteurize them, helping to prevent disease.

There are disadvantages to solar cookers, however. Food cannot be cooked on cloudy days, so a backup fuel-based system might be needed. Meals also take longer to cook in solar ovens. Thick foods like roasts can't be efficiently or safely cooked in solar cookers, so they must be cut into smaller pieces. Also, since some foods require special preparation techniques, traditional local dishes might have to be modified, or new cuisines introduced.

The Next Generation of Solar Technology

Researchers at the National Institute for Nanotechnology at the University of Alberta, Canada have discovered a way to create nanoparticles of zinc and phosphorus that absorb light and conduct electricity. These cheap, abundant materials can be used to make nanoparticle "inks" that can create solar cells in novel, mass-produced

Nanowires that are 1/10,000th the width of a human hair can boost the efficiency of solar cells.

ways similar to printing or spray-painting. Right now, the team has applied for a patent, and is experimenting with spray-coating large solar panels.

Nanowires Boost Efficiency

Nanowire crystals—cylinders of indium phosphate about 1/10,000th the width of a human hair—can be clustered on solar cells. These nanowires have certain properties that concentrate sunlight, resulting in much higher efficiency than silicon cells. Nanowire solar technology is still confined

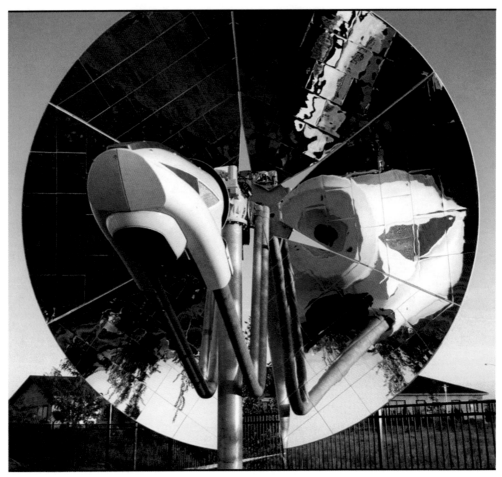

The Pacific Northwest National Laboratory in Washington State uses concentrated sunlight to convert natural gas to syngas, which allows natural gas power plants to use 20 percent less fuel to make electricity.

to the laboratory, but scientists hope it can soon be used for large-scale power stations.

Perovskite Solar Cells

A new kind of synthetic material called perovskite is showing promise for highly conductive solar cells. The particular crystalline structure of perovskites allows the electrons that are freed by solar radiation to travel farther without losing energy. This has resulted in up to 15 percent efficiency in solar panels constructed with perovskite. (A few years ago, 10 percent efficiency was considered an almost unattainable goal.)

Merging Solar and Natural Gas

The Department of Energy's Pacific Northwest National Laboratory has found a way to use solar energy to make natural gas more efficient. In their proposed new system, CSP solar heat is used to change natural gas into syngas. Syngas, or synthetic gas, is composed of hydrogen and carbon monoxide. Because it has a higher energy content than regular gas, a power plant can burn about 20 percent less syngas to produce the same amount of electricity.

Artificial Photosynthesis

In natural photosynthesis, a plant uses sunlight, water, and carbon dioxide to produce fuel in the form of carbohydrates and oxygen. In artificial photosynthesis, humans use sunlight and a catalyst to split water into its component molecules: oxygen and hydrogen. The hydrogen is then used as a fuel source. Also known as photocatalytic water splitting, this technology has the potential to provide abundant, clean, and cheap energy. When hydrogen is burned, it produces energy and water—not pollutants.

Previously, expensive metals such as platinum were used as catalysts. Recently, however, scientists developed a way to use the less efficient but vastly less expensive cobalt as part of the catalyst. Future studies will look at even more abundant materials such as nickel and iron. Because these substances are so readily available, artificial photosynthesis could occur on a massive scale. Some visionaries picture artificial photosynthesis facilities at all major coastal metropolises, splitting seawater to get hydrogen fuel. Others see a future where all man-made structures are retrofitted for artificial photosynthesis, converting even more energy from sunlight than all of the world's plant life.

The Future of Solar ... and the Planet

The Fifth Assessment Report of the Intergovernmental Panel on Climate Change, published in 2014, offers dire warnings for the future of our planet. Countries have been too reluctant to step up to the challenges of climate change, the report says. If another fifteen years pass without taking necessary steps to limit greenhouse gas emissions, the problem might become almost impossible to solve given our current level of technology. Despite the Kyoto Protocol and increased scientific awareness of the pollution caused by fossil fuels, governments are still subsidizing fossil fuel industries. Clean technologies like solar power are growing, but not nearly fast enough to offset the increase in fossil fuel use and greenhouse gas emissions in rapidly industrializing countries like China and India. Even with an international target of not allowing global warming to exceed

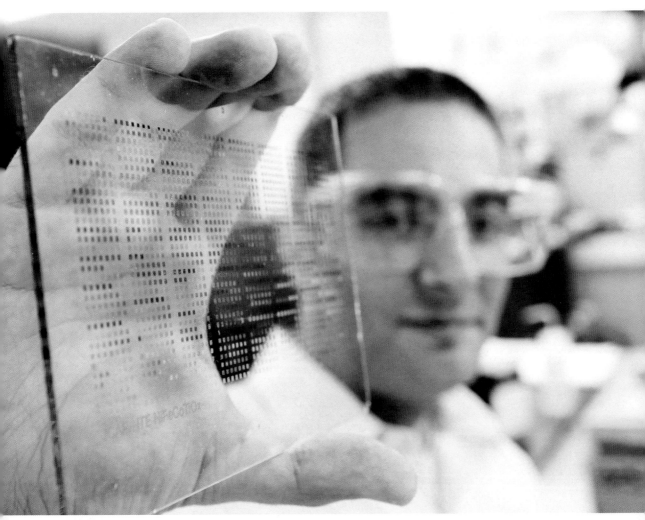

William Royea of the Joint Center for Artificial Photosynthesis at CalTech holds a test plate covered with different metal salts in an attempt to find the best substances for a new solar fuel generating device.

The future of solar energy
is in our hands.

3.6 degrees Fahrenheit (2 degrees Celsius) above what was maintained before the Industrial Revolution, when use of coal first began to harm the environment, there will still be great economic and environmental damage.

As technology improves, solar power has the potential to gradually replace fossil fuels. However, new technology has also allowed people to exploit previously unavailable fossil fuel resources, such as oil shale. Even if fossil fuels don't run out, the planet might not be able to survive their use.

In a world suffering the consequences of fossil fuels, solar energy presents an alternative that has the potential to power our planet cleanly and economically. Meanwhile, technology, industry, and infrastructure are struggling to help us reach that potential.

CRITICAL THINKING

- How do you think a person's life might change if they have a small amount of power, instead of none at all? What could they do with one light bulb at night, or an hour's worth of computer battery power?

- Plants give off water vapor. Can you come up with an invention for collecting fresh water from plants?

- What are some other advantages of not using biomass fuels in developing nations? What can happen to the environment when wood is the primary fuel? How long do you think it takes to gather enough biomass fuel every day? Who do you think does the gathering, and how might their lives change if their families use solar cookers instead?

- What are some of the major obstacles to putting the newest solar technologies into widespread use? How does something go from the laboratory to everyday applications?

Glossary

concentrated solar power (CSP): the process of using lenses or mirrors to focus and concentrate sunlight in one small area. The process can be used in everything from solar ovens to large-scale power plants.

electron: a subatomic, elementary particle with a negative electric charge

energy: power, or that which provides the capacity to do work

exajoule: a measurement of energy equal to one quintillion joules (A quintillion is 10 to the 18th power, or a one with eighteen zeros after it.)

greenhouse effect: the process by which solar radiation that passes through the atmosphere radiates back up to the greenhouse gases in the atmosphere, which absorb and then bounce back the thermal radiation in all directions. Some of the thermal radiation is sent back to Earth, increasing the temperature.

grid: an interconnected system to collect and distribute energy to municipalities

insolation: the measure of how much solar energy reaches the ground at any given time

joule: a unit of energy equal to the work required to exert one newton over a distance of one meter, or the energy required to pass an electrical current through a resistance of one ohm for one second, or the work required to produce one watt of power for one second

Glossary

kelvin: a temperature scale in which the zero is considered to be absolute zero, the temperature at which all motion ceases

kilowatt hour (kWh): a unit of energy measurement equal to 1,000 watt hours (3.6 megajoules). This unit is what appears on most household electric bills.

Kyoto Protocol: an international treaty that obligates industrialized nations to work to reduce greenhouse gas emissions

levelized cost: a per-kilowatt hour estimate of the cost of different kinds of power plants, taking into account the cost of the construction, fuel, maintenance, life expectancy, and estimated energy production for each power plant

megawatt hour (mWh): a unit of energy measurement equal to 1,000 kilowatt hours

non-renewable resource: a resource that does not replenish itself fast enough to be feasibly sustainable for human use. Some examples are fossil fuels like oil and coal.

nuclear fission: a nuclear reaction (or the result of radioactive decay) in which a nucleus splits, releasing energy

nuclear fusion: a process in which two nuclei collide and fuse, resulting in the production of energy in the form of photons

parabolic reflector: a reflective surface, such as a mirror, curved and set at a particular angle to concentrate the sun's rays

passive solar: a building design that takes advantage of the sun's location at different seasons to maximize climate control

photon: the elementary particle that is the quantum, or smallest possible part of light

photosynthesis: the process by which plants and some other organisms make energy from carbon dioxide and water, using the sun. This process produces oxygen

photovoltaic effect: the process by which a material exposed to light (sunlight or other light) produces an electrical current. Certain materials will absorb photons from light and release electrons, which are captured as voltage.

plasma: one of the four fundamental states of matter (the other three being gases, liquids, and solids). The sun is primarily plasma.

renewable resource: a natural resource that can replenish itself, such as sunlight or wind

semiconductor: a material that can conduct electricity, though not as well as metals, giving it properties that allow the electricity that passes through it to be more easily managed and captured

Find Out More

Books

Caduto, Michael J. *Catch the Wind, Harness the Sun*. North Adams, MA: Storey Publishing, 2011.

Haerens, Margaret, ed. *Energy Alternatives*. Farmington Hills, MI: Greenhaven Press, 2013.

Haugen, David M. and Susan Musser, eds. *Renewable Energy (Opposing Viewpoints)*. Farmington Hills, MI: Greenhaven Press, 2012.

Landau, Elaine. *The History of Energy*. Minneapolis, MN: Twenty-First Century Books, 2006.

Naff, Clay Farris, ed. *Solar Power*. Farmington Hills, MI: Greenhaven Press, 2007.

Websites

The Environmental Protection Agency
www.epa.gov

The EPA website offers a compendium of information about environmental issues, including global warming.

The National Renewable Energy Laboratory

www.nrel.gov

The NREL site presents the latest in clean energy information, including a copious amount of information on solar energy.

Renewable Energy World

www.renewableenergyworld.com

Find the latest news and blogs about all renewable energy sources at this website.

The U.S. Department of Energy

www.energy.gov

The official website of the cabinet department overseeing energy and nuclear technology features a wealth of information about energy consumer issues and the latest scientific discoveries.

The U.S. Energy Information Administration

www.eia.gov

You can find statistics and analysis of energy topics at the EIA website, with a special section for renewable energy.

Index

Page numbers in **boldface** are illustrations.

About the Author

Laura L. Sullivan is a prolific author of books for children and young adults. Her novels include the fantasies *Under the Green Hill* and *Guardian of the Green Hill*, as well as the historical novels *Ladies in Waiting* and *Love by the Morning Star*. She is also the author of Spotlight on Children's Authors: *Gail Carson Levine* for Cavendish Square. She lives on the west coast of sunny Florida, where she uses a solar clothes dryer (also known as a clothes line) and is investigating photovoltaic panels for her home.